Progressive Patterns
Decorative Designs
Adult Colouring Book

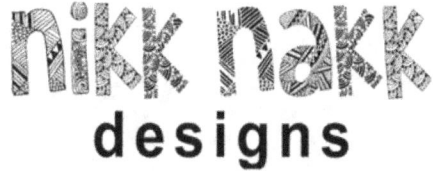

Progressive Patterns Decorative Designs - Adult Colouring Book
Copyright 2015 by nikk nakk designs
Created by Niki Palmer, Ros Tulleners
Illustrated by Stuart Campbell, Subrata Dutta, Elshan Gurbanov,

First edition 2015

ISBN: 978-1-925422-03-0

Welcome to the simple pleasure of colouring for adults.

Decorative Designs is the second book in the Progressive Patterns series, designed especially for the colorist who is looking for more challenging geometric designs.

Not sure how or where to start? All you really need are some coloured pencils and a good quality pencil sharpener to get started.

Take a chance and use our 'pot luck' method - it is so easy!
Make a up of tea or coffee if you need one.
Find a quiet place to work away from electronic distractions.
Let the book fall open at any page.
Close your eyes and pick up any colour.
Choose a shape and start to colour.
Woohoo ..... You are a colourist!

Soon you will be caught up in your work, your mind will be focused and the realities of the day will drift away. The tension will drain from your body as your pencils reveal the colourful masterpiece under your fingertips.. Try to allocate at least 15 -30 minutes a day to this simple, inexpensive way to calm your mind and body.

All you really need are some coloured pencils and a good quality pencil sharpener to get started. As your confidence and skill levels grow, you will be ready to experiment with more complex designs, different colouring techniques and begin to explore the amazing range of pencils, crayons, gel and metallic pens chalks and water colour effects - let your imagination run wild, there are no rules.

Most importantly, relax and have fun! The team at nikk nakk designs certainly had fun creating these designs for you to enjoy!

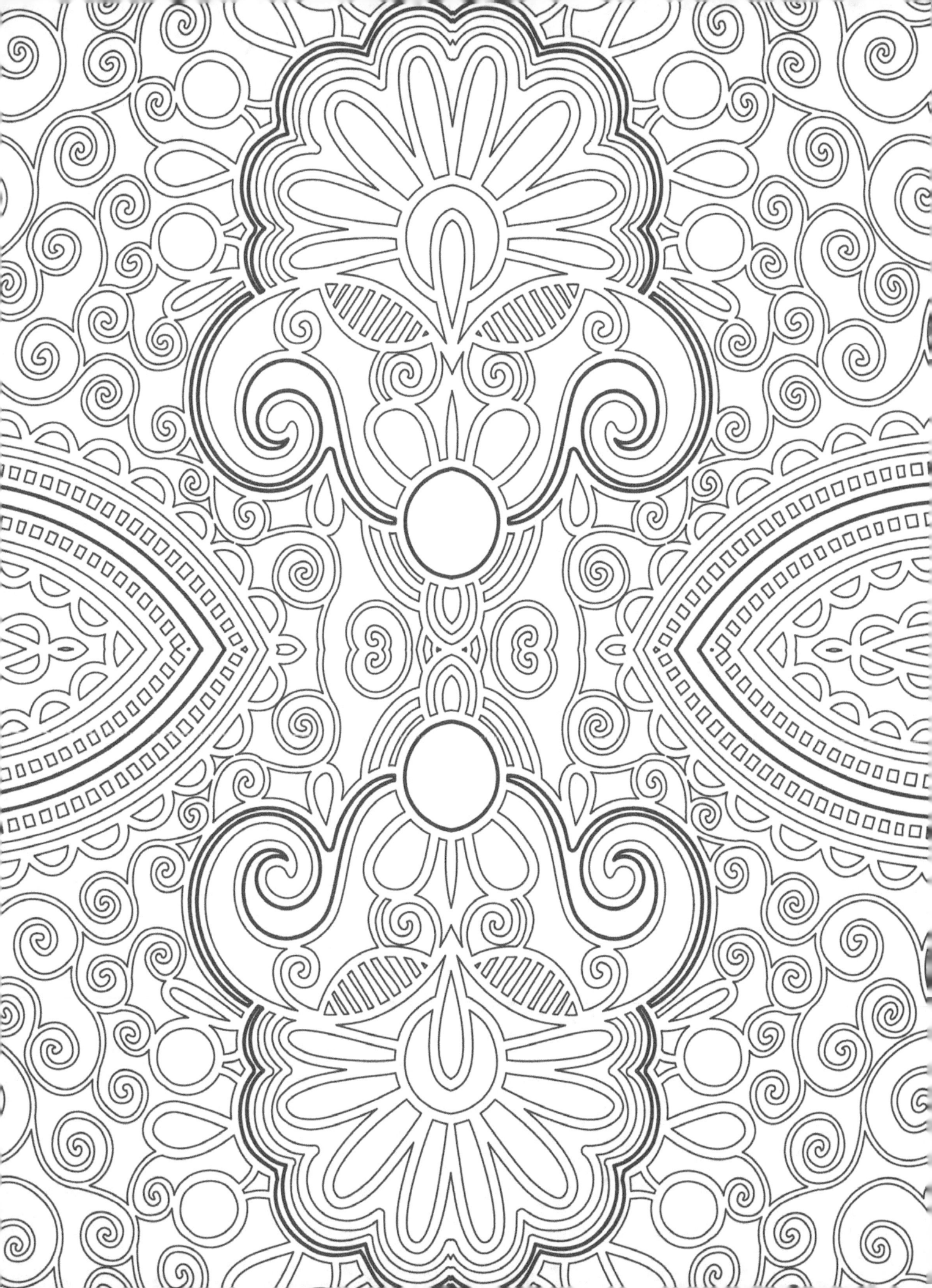

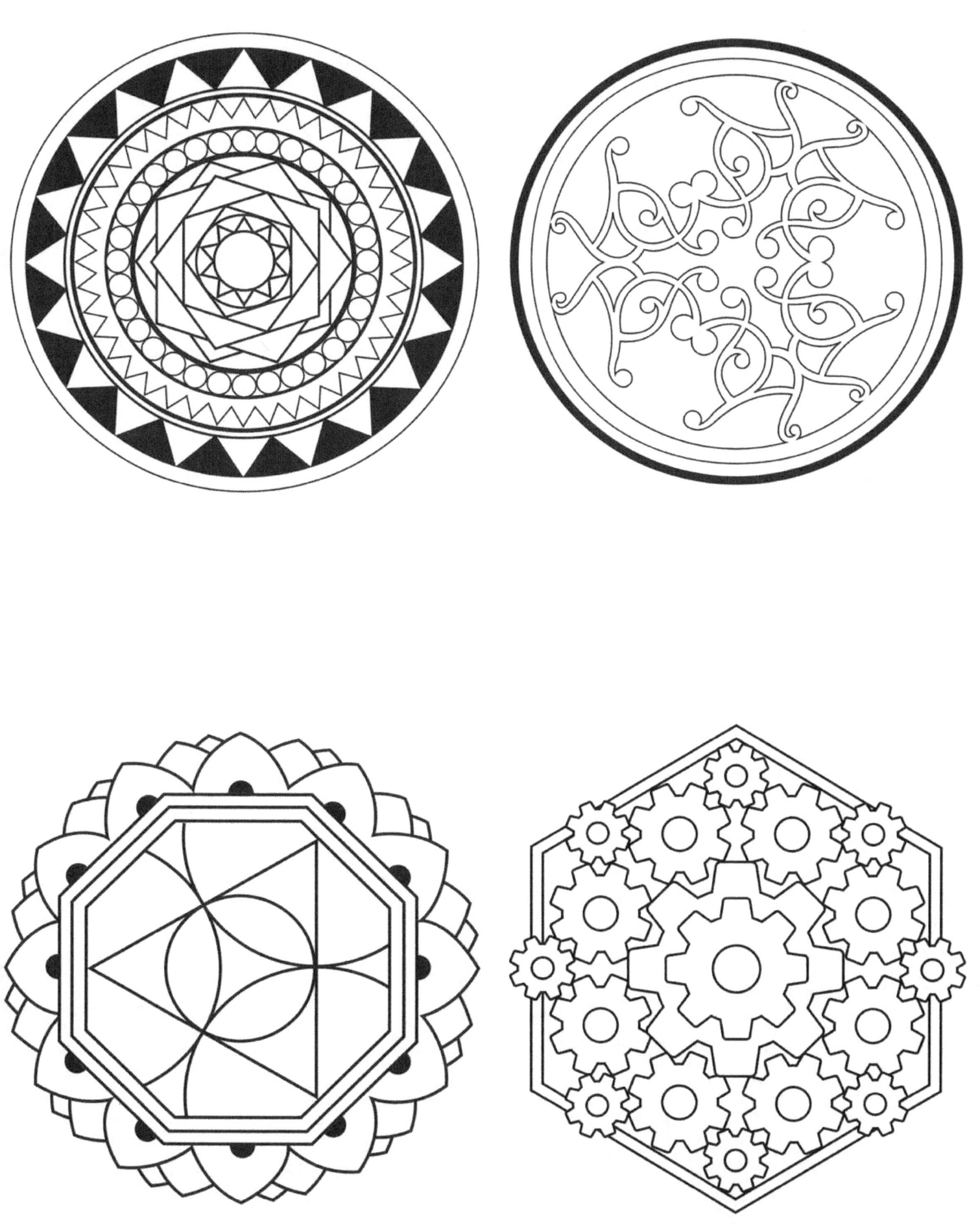

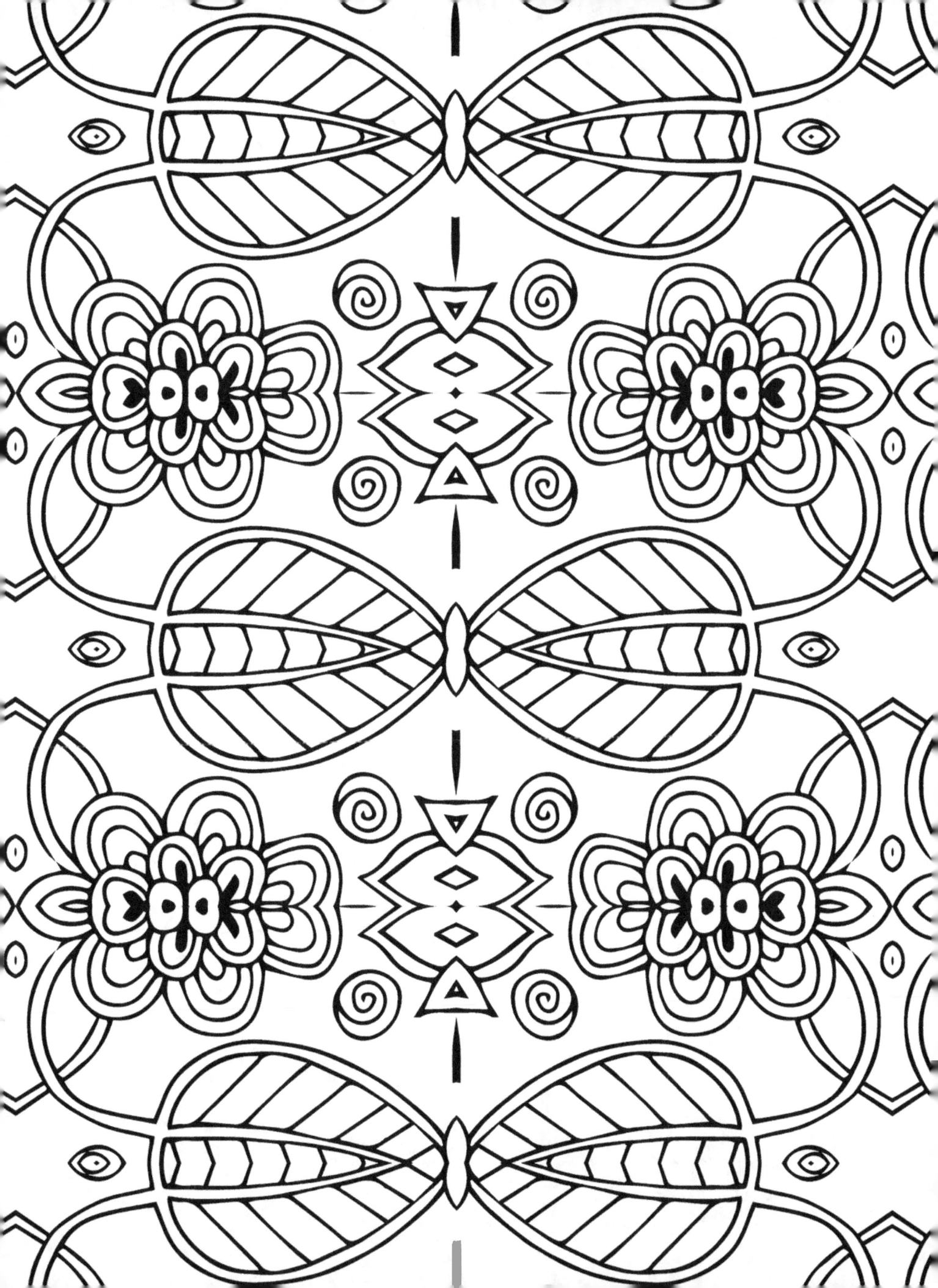

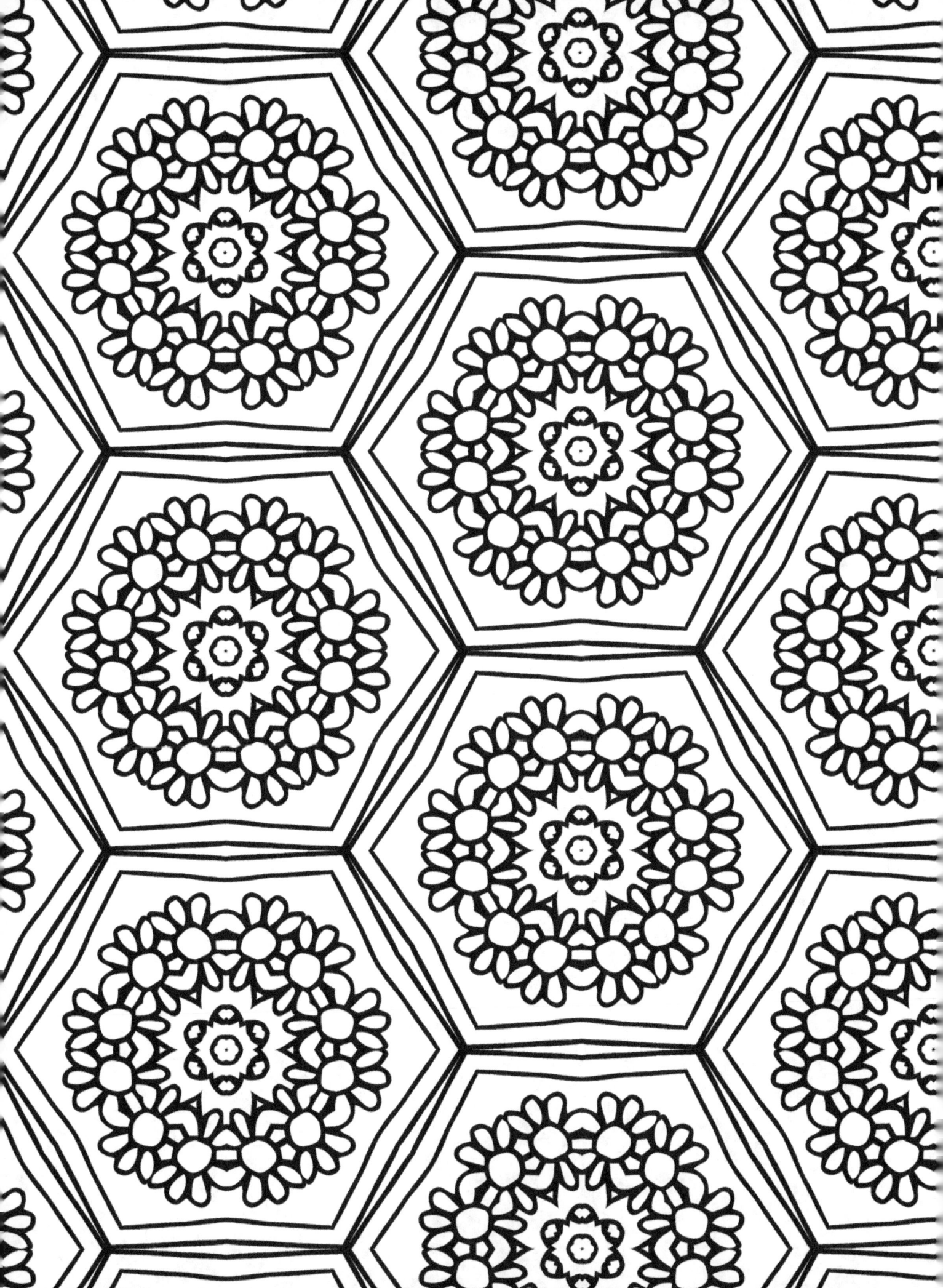

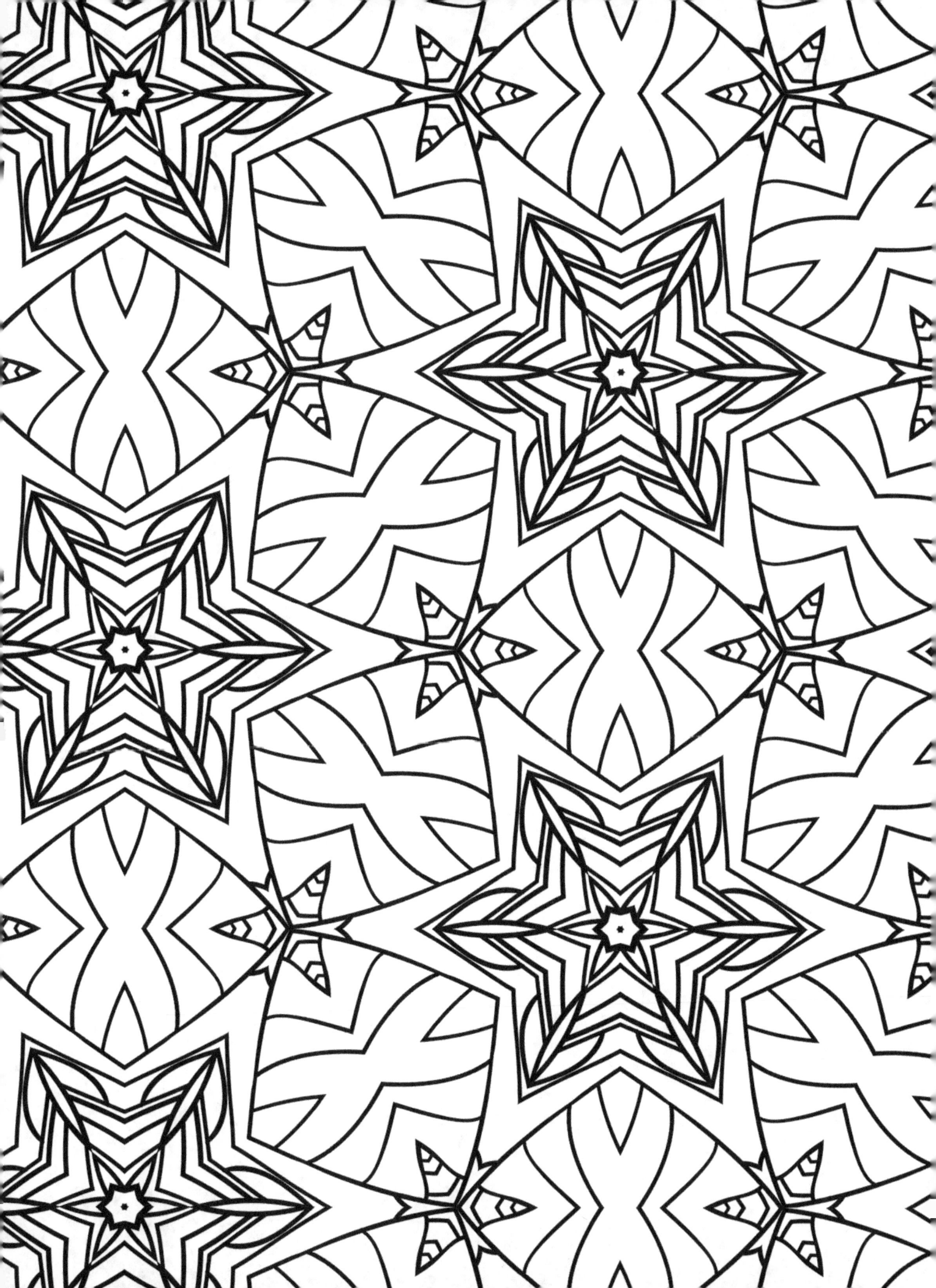

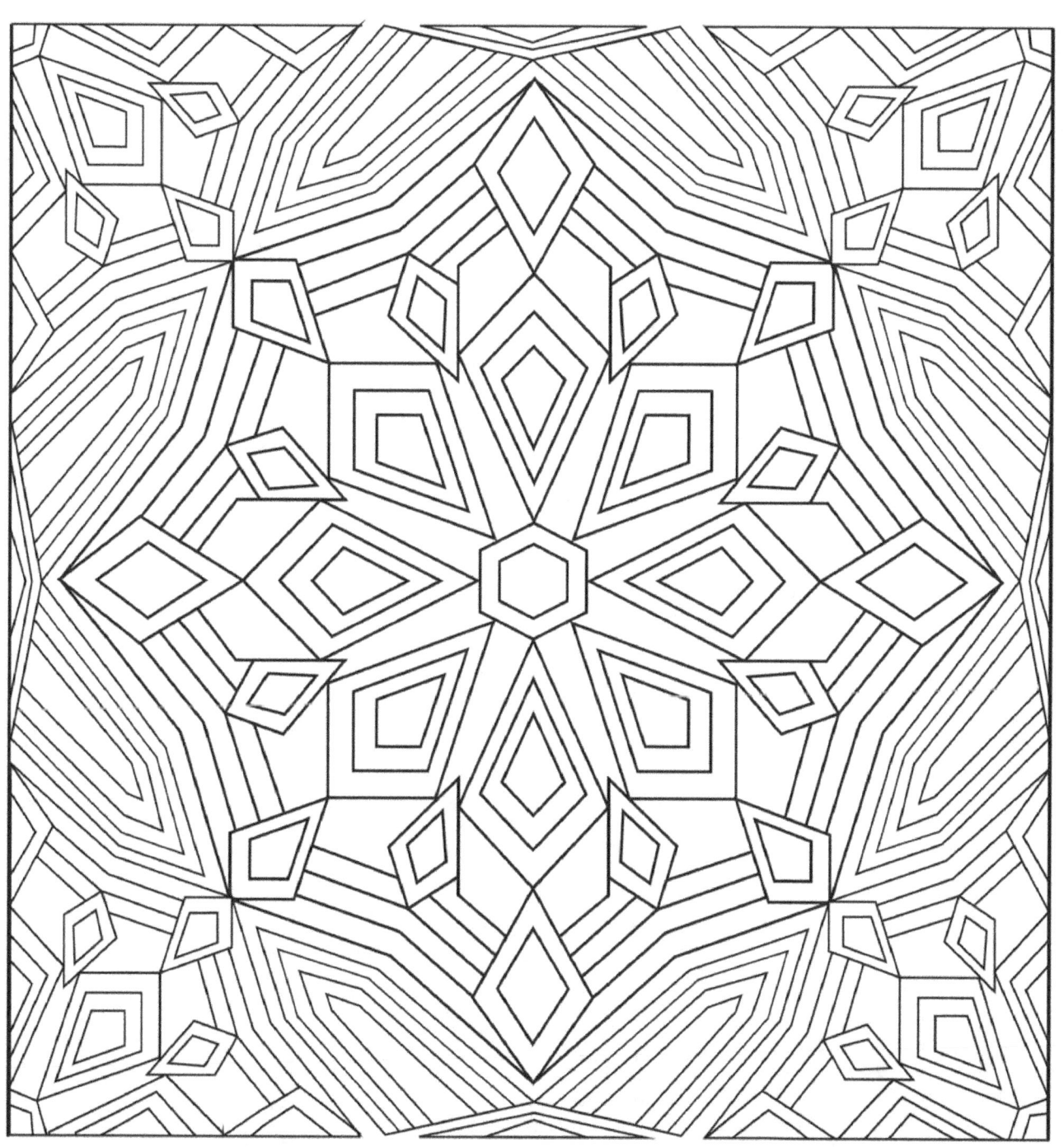

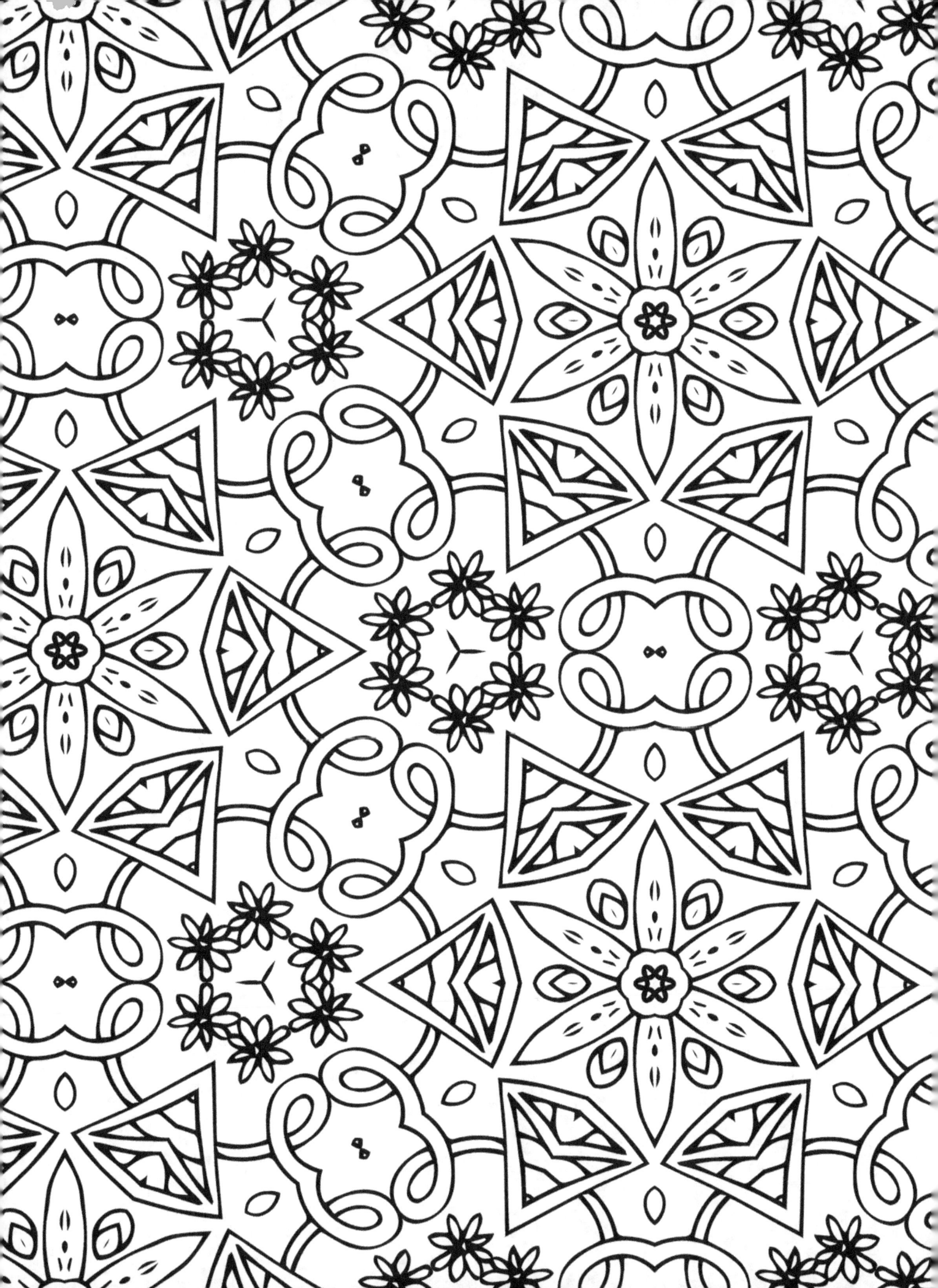

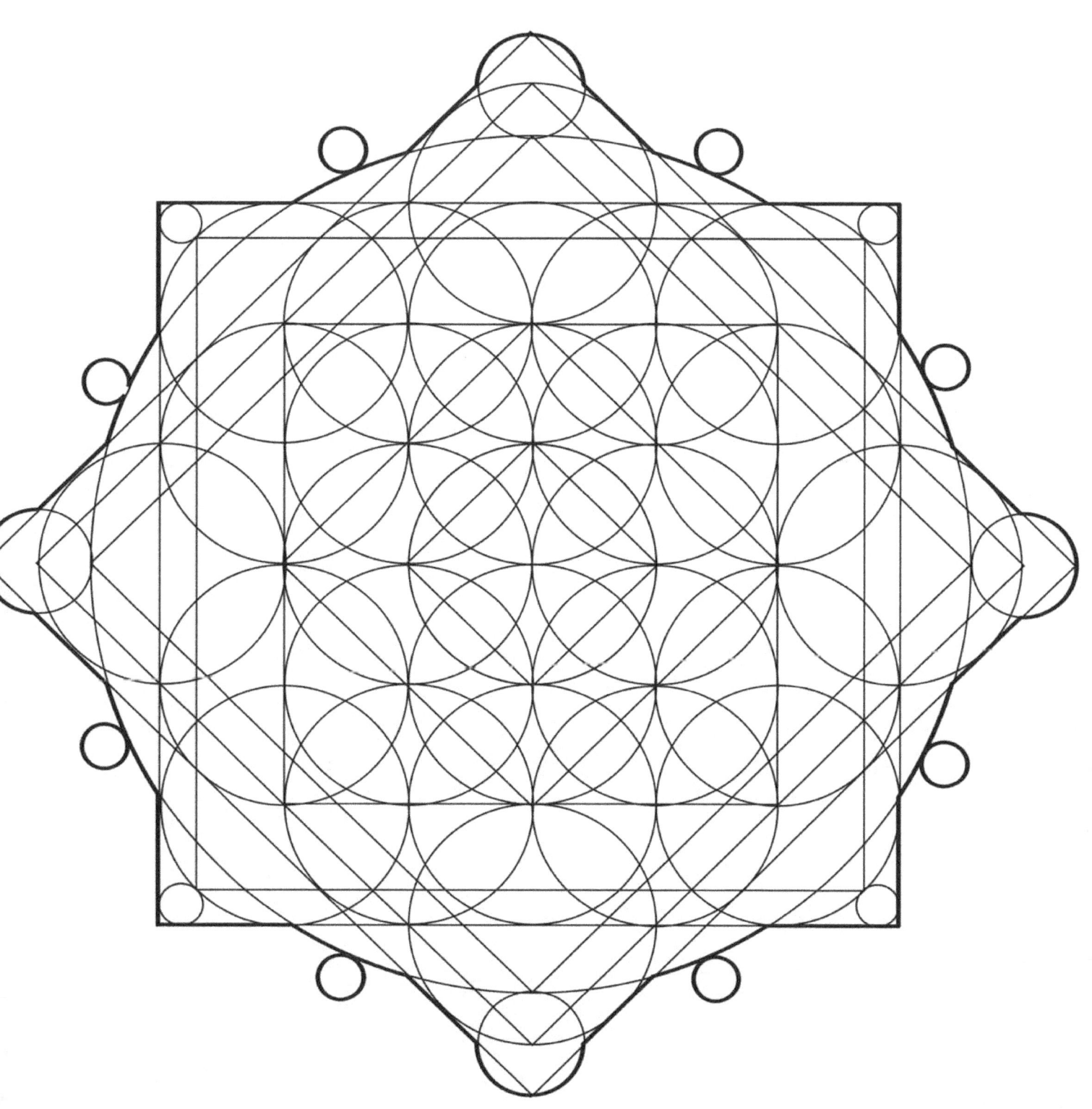

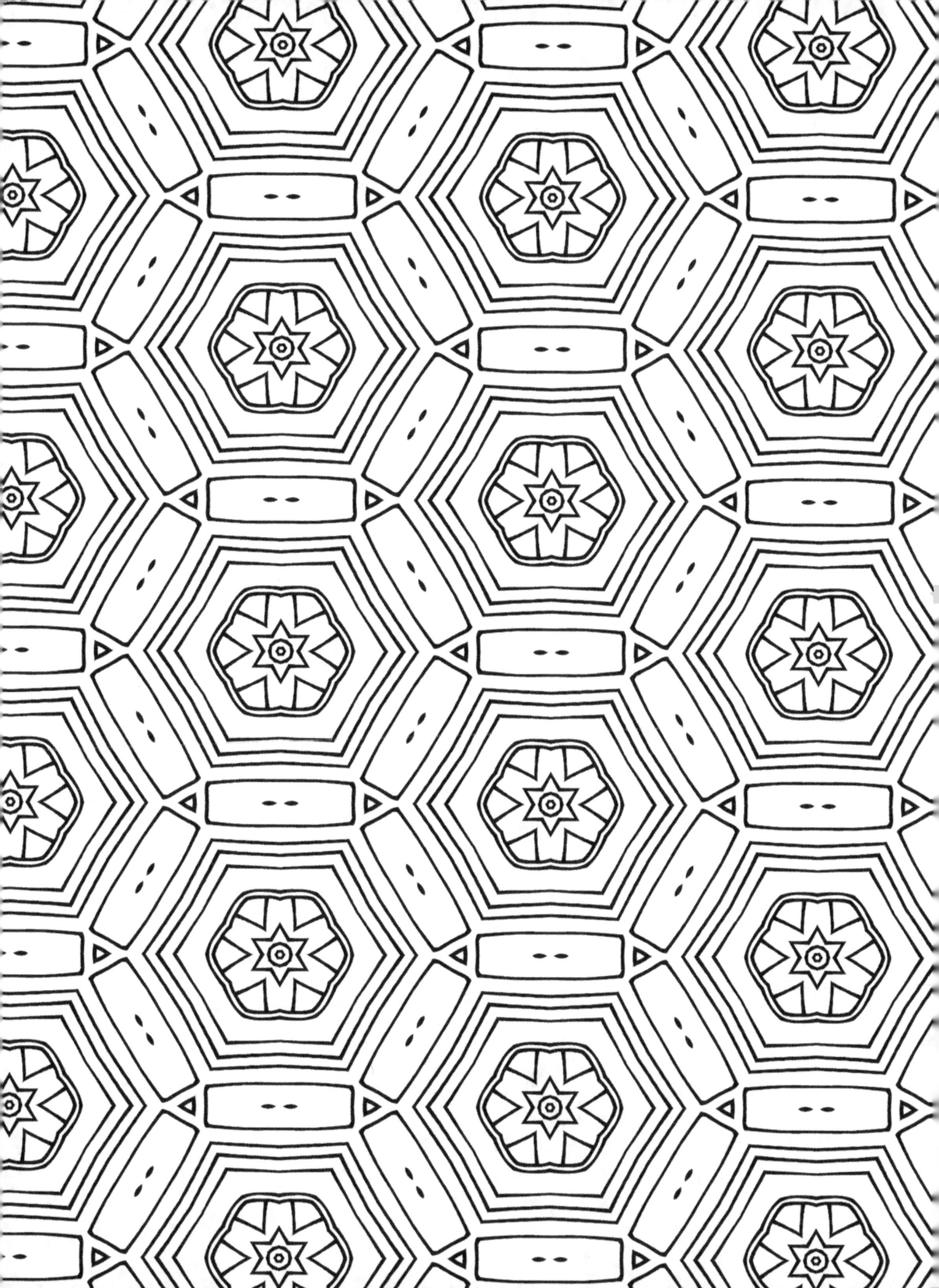

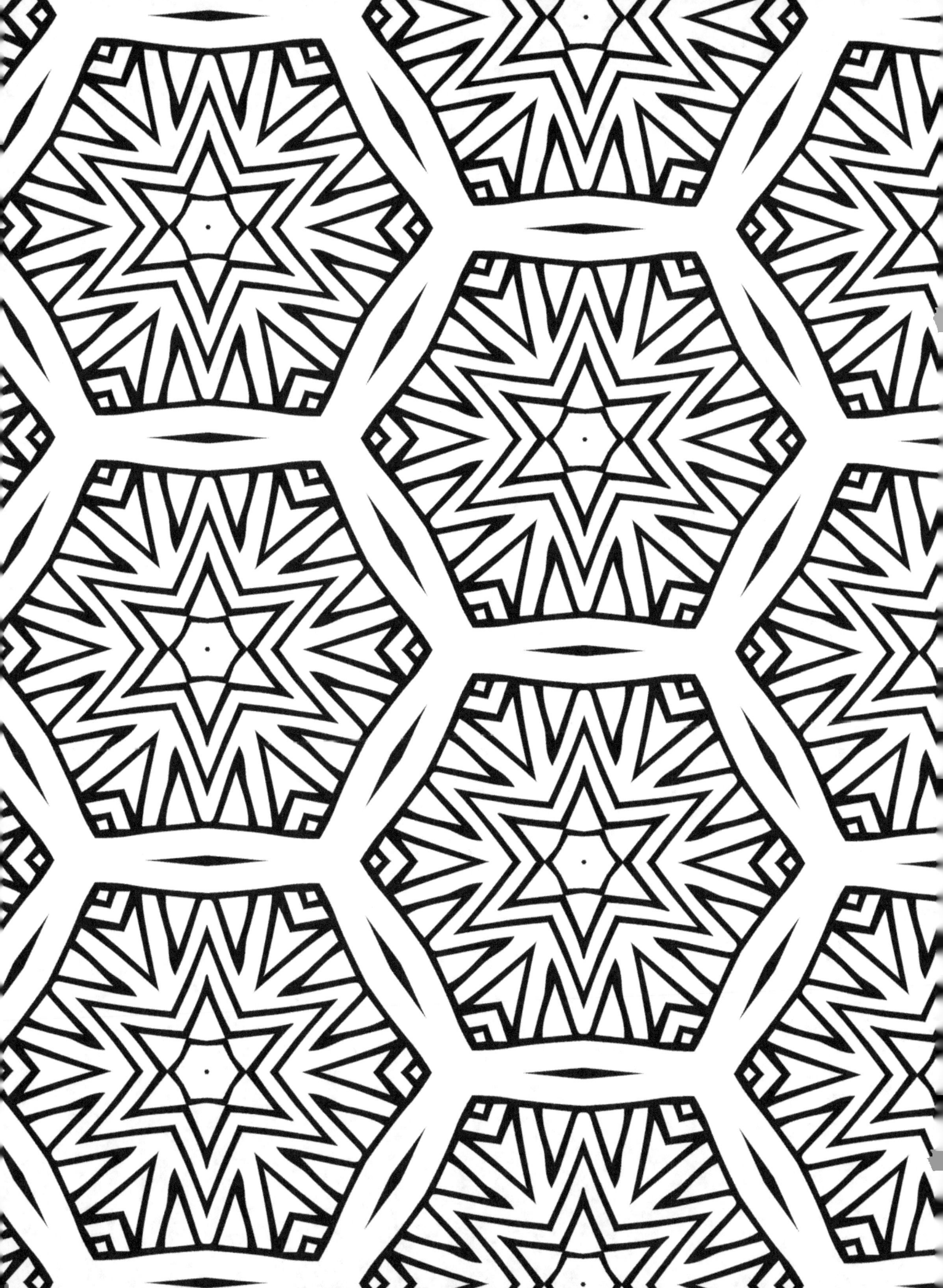

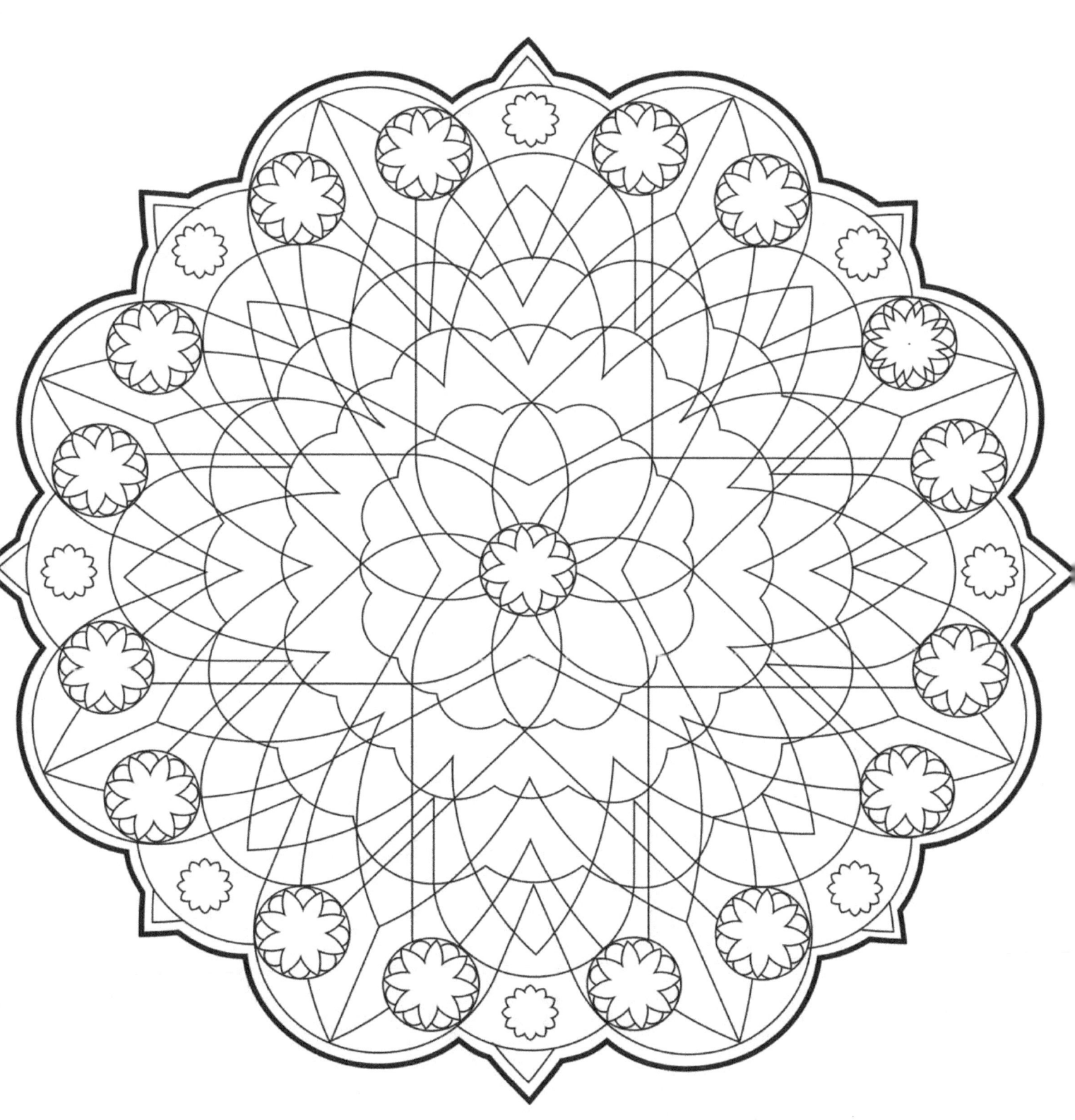

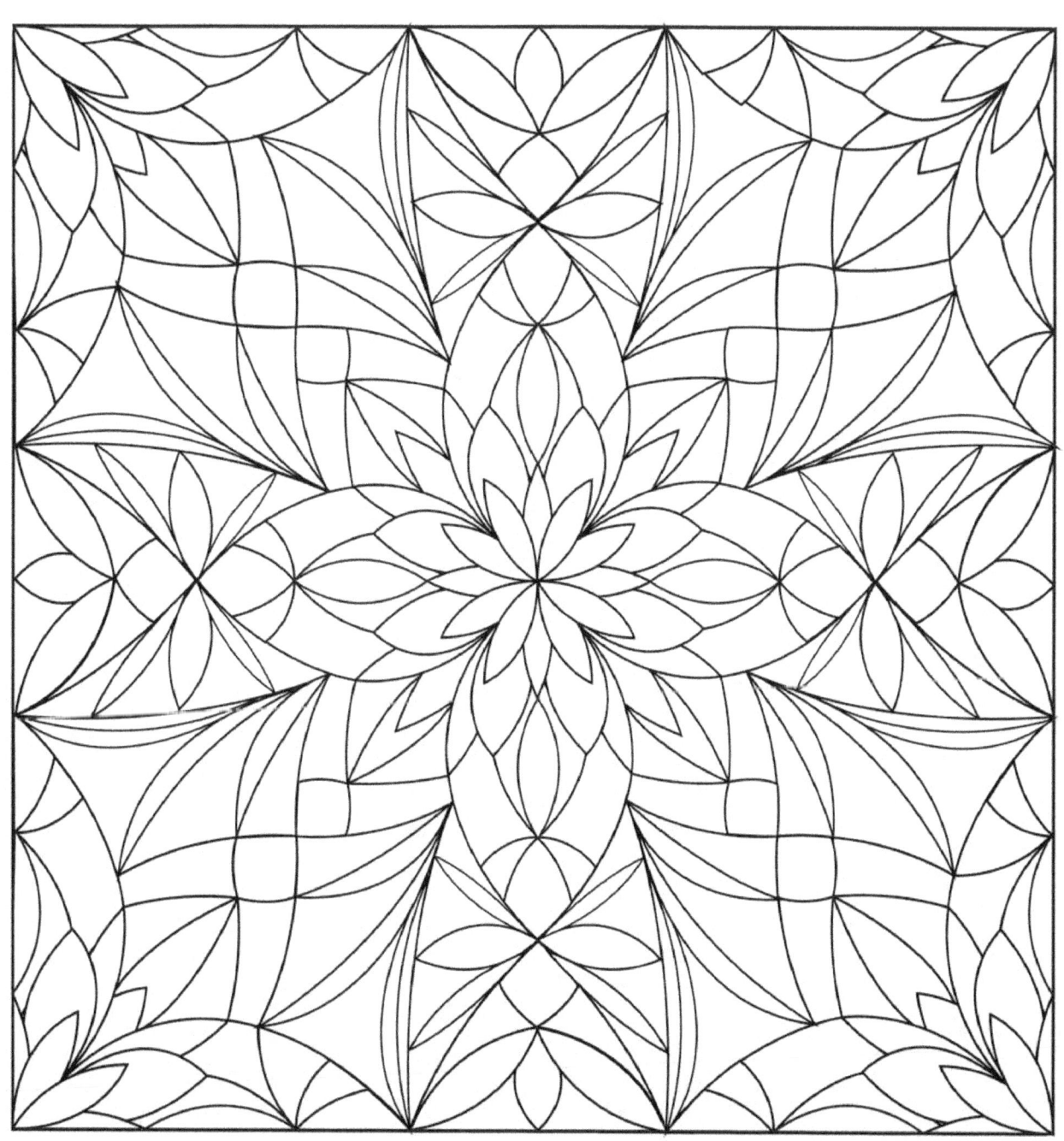

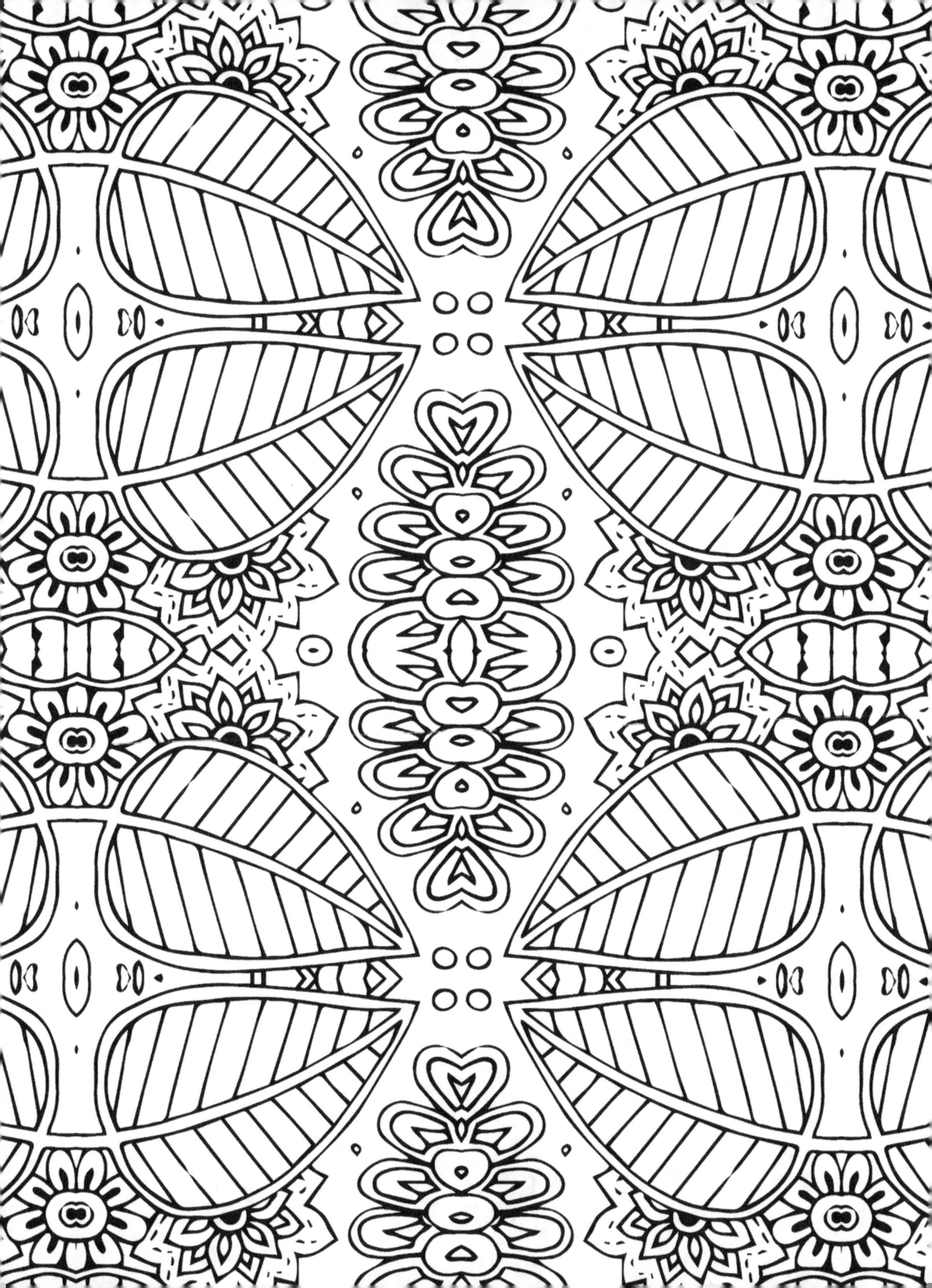

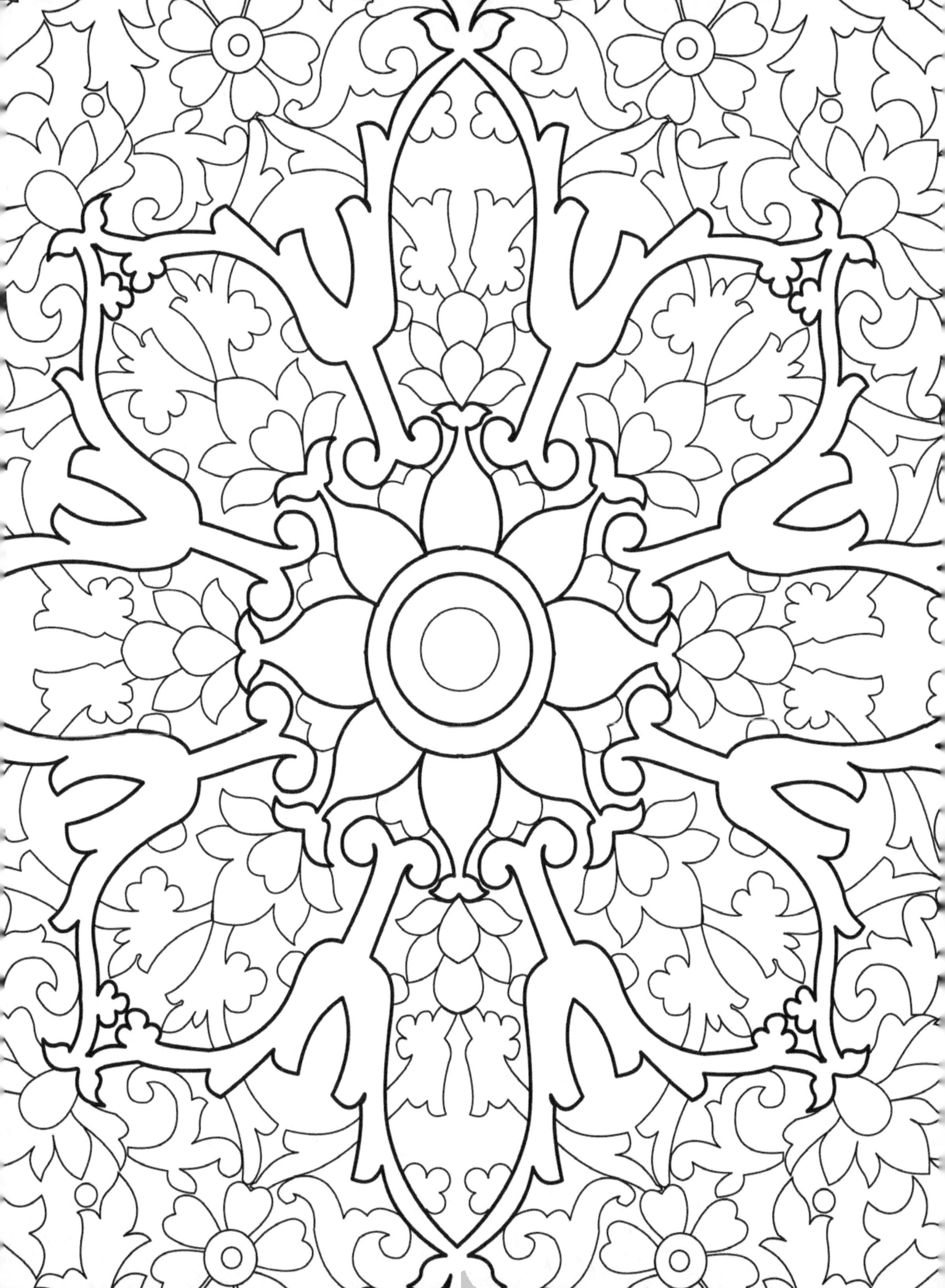

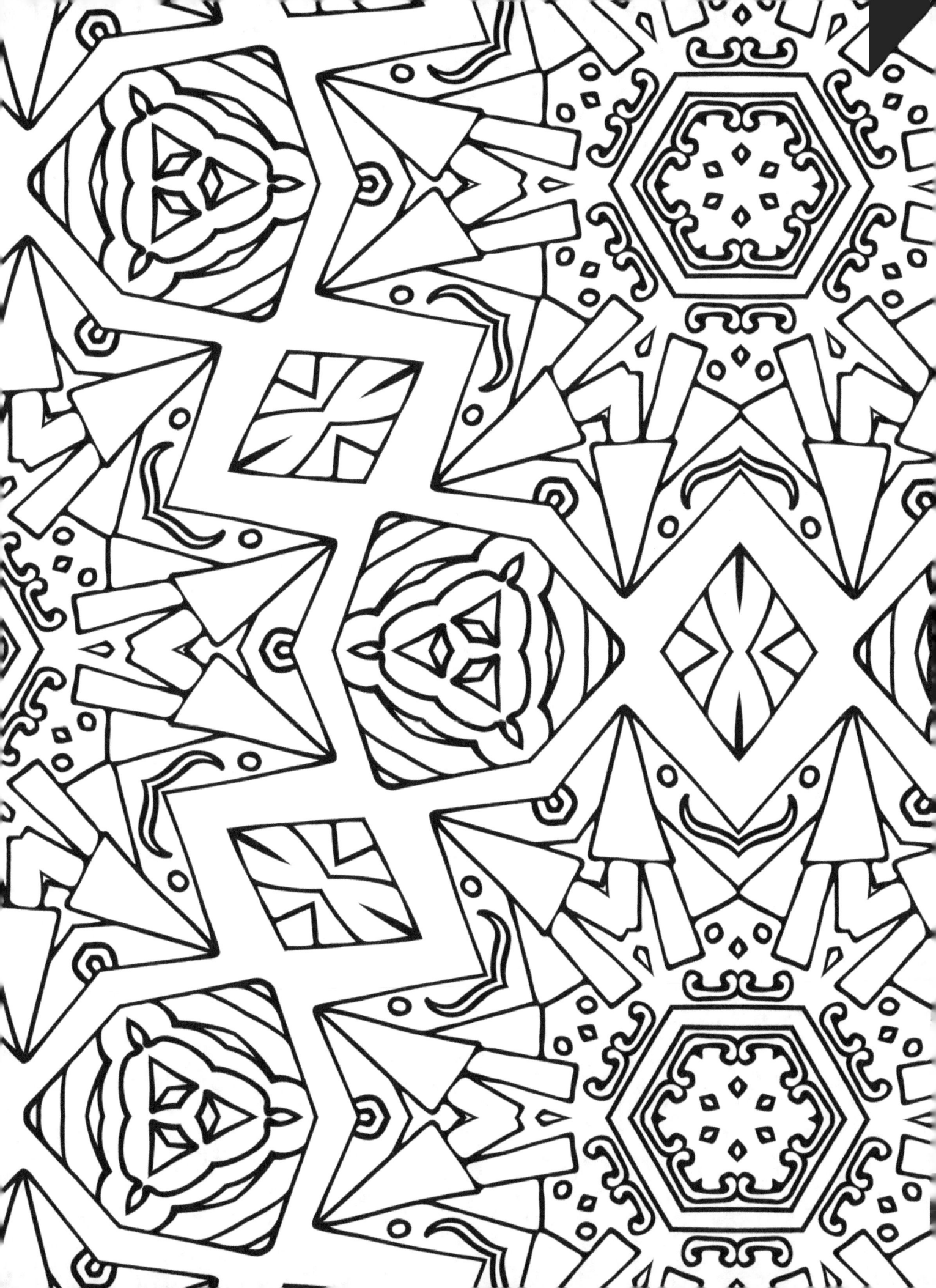

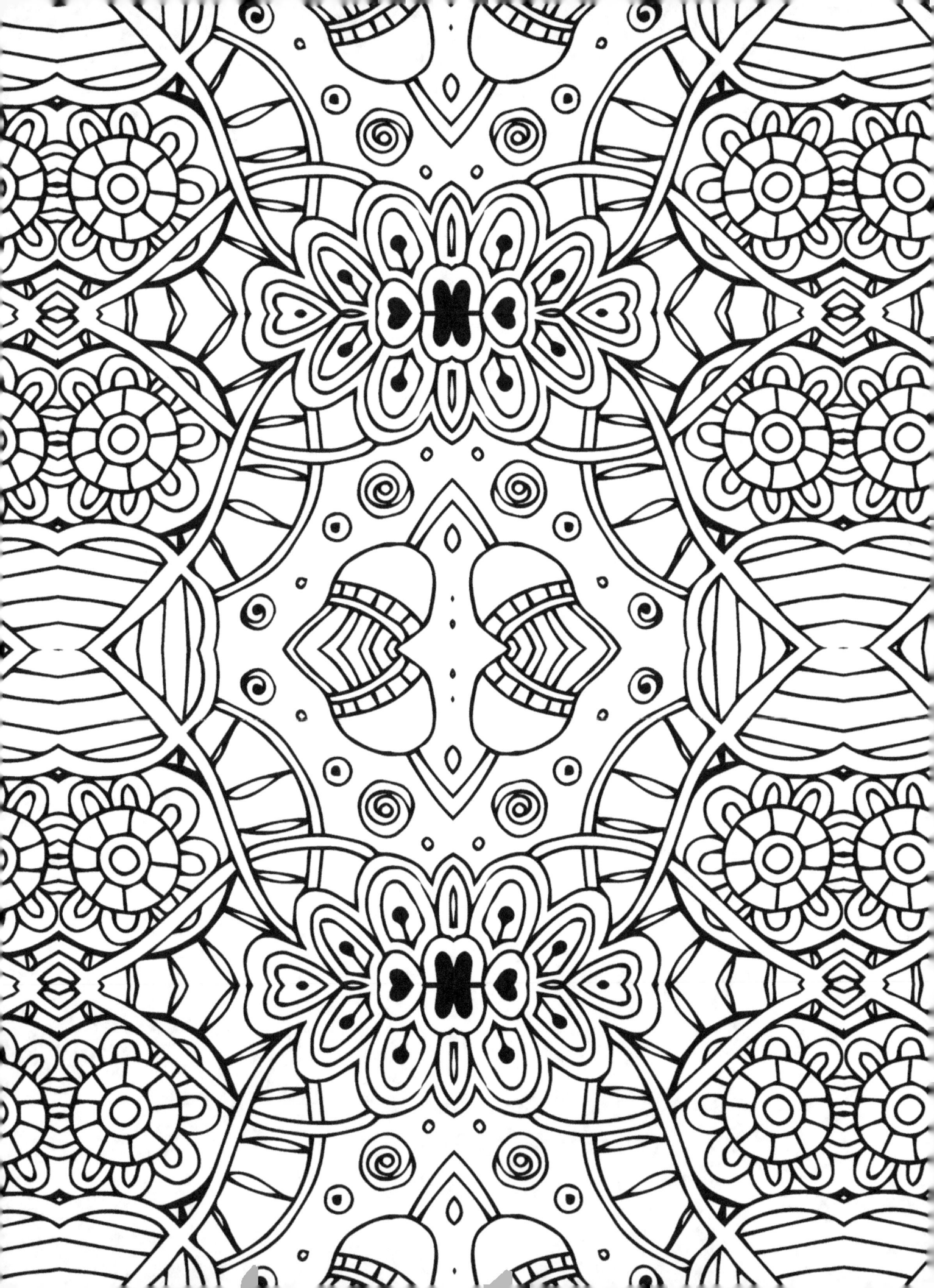

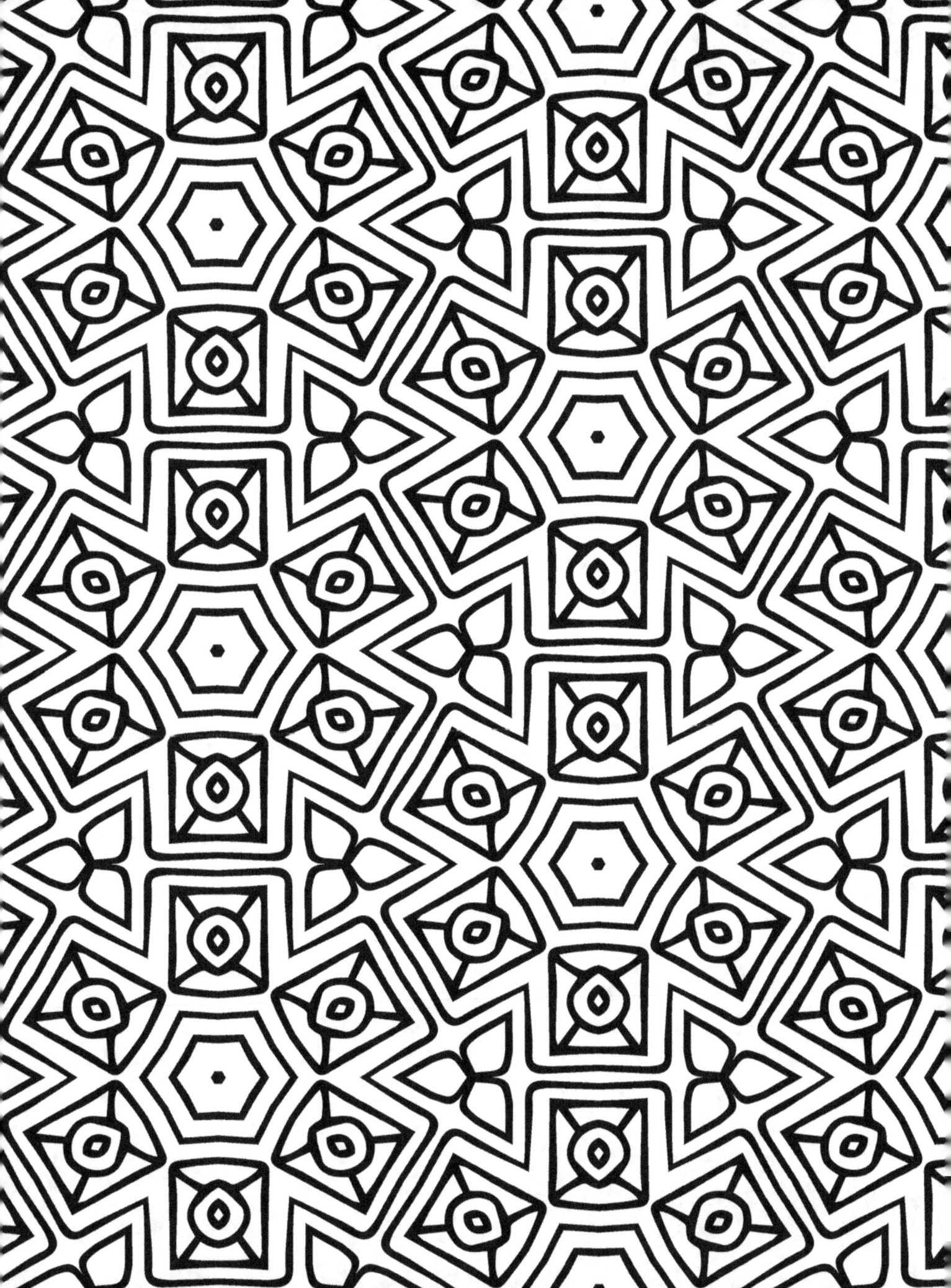

If you enjoyed colouring these designs, then move onto another book in the Progressive Patterns series of Adult Colouring Books.

We are sure you will love them!

We are amazed by the way that each of our designs looks so different when it has been coloured, so please share. We love to see your finished designs, don't be shy, head over to our Facebook page and show us what you have created.

https://www.facebook.com/progressivepatternsadultcolouringbooks

Look out for our other colouring books created by nikk nakk designs.

- Simple Styles
- Decorative Designs
- Intricate Inspirations
- Progressive Patterns Volume 1
- Progressive Patterns for Men
- Fairies and Flowers

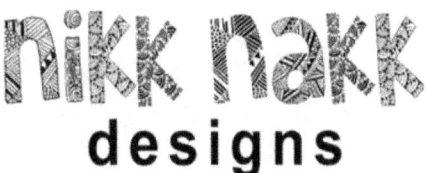

www.ingramcontent.com/pod-product-compliance
Lightning Source LLC
Chambersburg PA
CBHW081644220526

45468CB00009B/2551